incredibly easy
Vegetarian

Publications International, Ltd.
Favorite Brand Name Recipes at www.fbnr.com

Front cover photography and photography on pages 31, 61, 81, 83, 89, 91, 111, 125 and 127 by Chris Cassidy Photography, Inc.
Photographer: Chris Cassidy
Photographer's Assistant: Katie Stapely
Prop Stylist: Nancy Cassidy
Food Stylists: Kathy Aragaki, Lynn Gagne
Assistant Food Stylist: Sheila Grannon

Pictured on the front cover: Sesame Ginger-Glazed Tofu with Rice *(page 114).*
Pictured on the back cover: Barley and Pear-Stuffed Acorn Squash *(page 100).*

ISBN-13: 978-1-4127-9804-4
ISBN-10: 1-4127-9804-3

Library of Congress Control Number: 2009921764

Manufactured in China.

8 7 6 5 4 3 2 1

Microwave Cooking: Microwave ovens vary in wattage. Use the cooking times as guidelines and check for doneness before adding more time.

Preparation/Cooking Times: Preparation times are based on the approximate amount of time required to assemble the recipe before cooking, baking, chilling or serving. These times include preparation steps such as measuring, chopping and mixing. The fact that some preparations and cooking can be done simultaneously is taken into account. Preparation of optional ingredients and serving suggestions is not included.

Contents

Hummus with Garlic Pita
Chips (p. 10)

Refried Bean and Corn
Cakes (p. 15)

Fried Tofu with Sesame
Dipping Sauce (p. 6)

Edamame Hummus
(p. 20)

Small **Plates**

Fried Tofu with Sesame Dipping Sauce

3 tablespoons soy sauce or tamari
2 tablespoons unseasoned rice wine vinegar
2 teaspoons sugar
1 teaspoon sesame seeds, toasted*
1 teaspoon dark sesame oil
⅛ teaspoon red pepper flakes
1 package (14 ounces) extra firm tofu
2 tablespoons all-purpose flour
1 egg
¾ cup panko bread crumbs**
4 tablespoons vegetable oil, divided

To toast sesame seeds, spread seeds in small skillet. Shake skillet over medium-low heat until seeds begin to pop and turn golden, about 3 minutes.

**Panko bread crumbs are used in Japanese cooking to provide a crisp exterior to fried foods. They are coarser than ordinary bread crumbs.*

1. For dipping sauce, combine soy sauce, vinegar, sugar, sesame seeds, sesame oil and red pepper flakes in small bowl. Set aside.

2. Drain tofu and press between paper towels to remove excess water. Cut crosswise into 4 slices; cut each slice diagonally into triangles. Place flour in shallow dish. Beat egg in shallow bowl. Place panko in another shallow bowl.

3. Dip each piece of tofu in flour to lightly coat all sides; dip in egg, turning to coat. Drain; roll in panko to coat lightly.

4. Heat 2 tablespoons vegetable oil in large nonstick skillet over high heat. Reduce heat to medium; add half of tofu in single layer. Cook 1 to 2 minutes per side or until golden brown. Repeat with remaining tofu. Serve with dipping sauce.   *Makes 4 to 8 servings*

Barley "Caviar"

4 cups water
½ teaspoon salt, divided
¾ cup uncooked pearled barley
½ cup sliced pimiento-stuffed olives
½ cup finely chopped red bell pepper
1 stalk celery, chopped
1 large shallot, finely chopped
1 jalapeño pepper,* minced *or* ¼ teaspoon red
 pepper flakes
2 tablespoons plus 1 teaspoon olive oil
4 teaspoons white wine vinegar
¼ teaspoon ground cumin
⅛ teaspoon black pepper
8 leaves endive or Bibb lettuce

*Jalapeño peppers can sting and irritate the skin, so wear rubber gloves when handling peppers and do not touch your eyes.

1. Bring water and ¼ teaspoon salt to a boil in medium saucepan over high heat. Stir in barley. Cover; reduce heat to low. Simmer 45 minutes or until tender. Remove from heat; let stand 5 minutes. Rinse under cold water; drain well. Place in large bowl.

2. Stir in olives, bell pepper, celery, shallot and jalapeño. Stir together oil, vinegar, remaining ¼ teaspoon salt, cumin and black pepper in small bowl. Pour over barley mixture; stir gently to mix well. Let stand 10 minutes.

3. To serve, spoon barley mixture evenly into endive leaves.

Makes 8 servings

Hummus with Garlic Pita Chips

Prep Time: 5 minutes • **Start to Finish Time:** 15 minutes

Hummus
   2 tablespoons POLANER® Chopped Garlic
   1 (16-ounce) can chickpeas, drained
   ¼ cup fresh cilantro
   **¼ cup CREAM OF WHEAT® Hot Cereal (Instant, 1-minute,
      2½-minute or 10-minute cook time), uncooked**
   2 tablespoons tahini*
   2 tablespoons lemon juice
   ½ teaspoon salt
   ½ teaspoon ground black pepper
   ¾ cup olive oil

Garlic Pita Chips
   **2 tablespoons CREAM OF WHEAT® Hot Cereal (Instant,
      1-minute, 2½-minute or 10-minute cook time), uncooked**
   1 teaspoon garlic salt
   4 pita breads
   Nonstick cooking spray

Tahini is a thick, mild-flavored, light-colored paste made from ground sesame seeds and used in Middle Eastern dishes. It can usually be found in the supermarket ethnic foods aisle.

1. Place garlic in food processor; pulse several times. Add chickpeas, cilantro, Cream of Wheat, tahini, lemon juice, salt and pepper; pulse several more times. While food processor is running, slowly pour in olive oil until dip thickens.

2. Prepare pita chips. Preheat oven to 350°F. Combine Cream of Wheat and garlic salt in small bowl; set aside.

3. Cut pita breads into 12 wedges each. Arrange in single layer on baking sheet. Spray generously with nonstick cooking spray. Sprinkle Cream of Wheat mixture onto chips. Bake 6 minutes. Turn chips over; bake 6 minutes longer. Serve with hummus.   *Makes 6 to 12 servings*

Tip: Hummus makes a great spread. Add to sandwiches, pita breads or wraps stuffed with fresh vegetables.

Toasted Ravioli with Spicy Red Sauce

1 package (about 9 ounces) refrigerated cheese ravioli
Nonstick cooking spray
½ cup plain dry bread crumbs
¼ cup grated Parmesan cheese
1 teaspoon dried basil
1 teaspoon dried oregano
¼ teaspoon black pepper
2 egg whites
Prepared salsa or spicy pasta sauce

1. Cook ravioli according to package directions. Rinse under cold running water until ravioli are cool; drain well.

2. Preheat oven to 375°F. Spray baking sheet with cooking spray. Combine bread crumbs, cheese, basil, oregano and pepper in medium bowl.

3. Beat egg whites lightly in shallow dish. Add ravioli; toss lightly to coat. Transfer ravioli, a few at a time, to bread crumb mixture; toss to coat evenly. Arrange in single layer on prepared baking sheet. Spray tops of ravioli with cooking spray.

4. Bake 12 to 14 minutes or until crisp. Serve ravioli with pasta sauce for dipping. *Makes 8 servings*

Toasted Artichoke Ravioli: Substitute 1 package (about 9 ounces) refrigerated artichoke & cheese ravioli for cheese ravioli. Prepare as directed above.

Crispy Onion Veggies

Prep Time: 10 minutes • **Cook Time:** 10 minutes

1⅓ cups *French's*® French Fried Onions or *French's*® Cheddar French Fried Onions
¼ cup all-purpose flour
1 to 2 medium zucchini, cut diagonally into ¼-inch slices
1 egg, beaten

1. Crush French Fried Onions in plastic bag using hands or rolling pin.

2. Place flour into separate bag. Toss zucchini in flour; shake off excess.

3. Dip zucchini pieces into beaten egg; then toss in crushed onions, a few pieces at a time.

4. Arrange zucchini on greased rack set over rimmed baking sheet. Bake at 400°F for 10 minutes or until tender. *Makes 6 servings*

Crispy Onion Mushrooms: Substitute one 10-ounce package whole button mushrooms. Proceed as above.

Crunchy Double Onion Rings: Crush 2 cups French Fried Onions in plastic bag and toss with 2 tablespoons flour; set aside. Slice 2 large onions into ½-inch thick rings. Coat onion rings in ¼ cup flour. Dip into 2 beaten egg whites, then into crushed French Fried Onion mixture. Bake according to recipe above.

Bite-You-Back Roasted Edamame

2 teaspoons vegetable oil
2 teaspoons honey
¼ teaspoon wasabi powder*
1 package (10 ounces) shelled edamame, thawed if frozen
Kosher salt

*Available in the Asian section of most supermarkets and in Asian specialty markets.

1. Preheat oven to 375°F.

2. Combine oil, honey and wasabi powder in large bowl; mix well. Add edamame; toss to coat. Spread on baking sheet in single layer.

3. Bake 12 to 15 minutes or until golden brown, stirring once. Immediately remove from baking sheet to large bowl; sprinkle generously with salt. Cool completely before serving. Store in airtight container.

Makes 4 to 8 servings

Refried Bean and Corn Cakes

Prep Time: 10 minutes • **Start to Finish:** 20 minutes

1 can (16 ounces) ORTEGA® Refried Beans
1 cup crushed ORTEGA® Taco Shells
1 egg
1 tablespoon ORTEGA® Fire-Roasted Diced Green Chiles
¼ cup vegetable or corn oil
½ cup ORTEGA® Black Bean and Corn Salsa
Sour cream (optional)
Chopped fresh cilantro (optional)

Combine refried beans, taco shells, egg and chiles in large mixing bowl; stir well. Let stand 5 minutes.

Heat oil in large skillet. Drop bean mixture into pan by heaping tablespoonfuls; do not crowd pan. Mash into flat cakes with spatula. Fry cakes about 4 minutes; turn over and fry 4 minutes longer. Drain on paper towels. Cook remaining bean mixture in batches.

Spoon sour cream, if desired, and 1 tablespoon salsa on each cake. Garnish with cilantro, if desired. Serve warm or at room temperature.

Makes 6 to 8 servings

Garden Ratatouille

2 tablespoons extra-virgin olive oil
1 cup chopped sweet onion
1 yellow or red bell pepper, cut into ½-inch cubes
4 cloves garlic, minced
1 medium eggplant (about 12 ounces), peeled, cut into ½-inch cubes
1 can (about 14 ounces) Italian-style stewed tomatoes, coarsely chopped
⅓ cup sliced pitted kalamata or black olives
1 tablespoon plus 1½ teaspoons balsamic vinegar
½ teaspoon salt
¼ teaspoon red pepper flakes
¼ cup chopped fresh basil or Italian parsley
8 slices French bread

1. Heat oil in large deep skillet over medium heat. Add onion; cook and stir 5 minutes. Add bell pepper and garlic; cook and stir 5 minutes. Stir in eggplant, tomatoes and olives. Bring to a boil over high heat. Reduce heat; simmer, covered, 15 minutes or until vegetables are tender.

2. Stir in vinegar, salt and pepper flakes; cook, uncovered, 2 minutes. Remove from heat; stir in basil. Serve warm or at room temperature on toasted French bread slices. *Makes 8 servings*

Note: Ratatouille is a classic vegetable stew from the Provence region of France. Traditionally, it is served as a side dish.

Spicy Polenta Cheese Bites

3 cups water
1 cup corn grits
½ teaspoon salt
¼ teaspoon chili powder
1 tablespoon butter
¼ cup minced onion or shallot
1 tablespoon minced jalapeño pepper*
½ cup (2 ounces) shredded sharp Cheddar cheese or fontina cheese

*Jalapeño peppers can sting and irritate the skin, so wear rubber gloves when handling peppers and do not touch your eyes.

1. Grease 8-inch square pan; set aside. Bring water to a boil in large nonstick saucepan over high heat. Slowly add grits, stirring constantly. Reduce heat to low. Cook, stirring frequently, until grits are tender and water is absorbed. Stir in salt and chili powder.

2. Melt butter in small saucepan over medium-high heat. Add onion and jalapeño; cook and stir 3 to 5 minutes or until tender. Stir into grits; mix well. Spread in prepared pan. Let stand 1 hour or until cool and firm.

3. Set broiler rack 4 inches from heat; preheat broiler. Cut polenta into 16 squares; sprinkle with cheese. Carefully lift out squares; arrange on nonstick baking sheet. Broil 5 minutes or until cheese is melted and slightly browned. Remove immediately. Cut each square in half. (Polenta will firm as it cools.)   *Makes 32 appetizers*

Tip: For spicier flavor, add ⅛ to ¼ teaspoon red pepper flakes to the onion-jalapeño mixture.

Edamame Hummus

1 package (16 ounces) frozen shelled edamame, thawed
2 green onions, coarsely chopped (about ½ cup)
½ cup loosely packed fresh cilantro
3 to 4 tablespoons water
2 tablespoons canola oil
1½ tablespoons fresh lime juice
1 tablespoon honey
2 cloves garlic
1 teaspoon salt
¼ teaspoon black pepper
Rice crackers, baby carrots, cucumber slices and sugar snap peas

1. Combine edamame, green onions, cilantro, 3 tablespoons water, oil, lime juice, honey, garlic, salt and pepper in food processor; process until smooth. Add additional water to thin dip, if necessary.

2. Serve with crackers and vegetables for dipping. Store leftover dip in refrigerator for up to 4 days.   *Makes about 2 cups*

*Tip

Edamame are fresh, green soybeans with a mild flavor and a firm, smooth texture. Thawed frozen shelled edamame are a delicious addition to soups, chilis, pasta and rice dishes.

Asian Vegetable Rolls with Soy-Lime Dipping Sauce

Prep Time: 15 minutes

¼ **cup soy sauce**
2 **tablespoons lime juice**
1 **teaspoon honey**
1 **clove garlic, crushed**
½ **teaspoon finely chopped fresh ginger**
¼ **teaspoon dark sesame oil**
⅛ **to ¼ teaspoon red pepper flakes**
½ **cup grated cucumber**
⅓ **cup grated carrot**
¼ **cup sliced yellow bell pepper (1 inch long)**
2 **tablespoons thinly sliced green onion**
18 **small lettuce leaves or Bibb lettuce leaves from inner part of head**
   Sesame seeds (optional)

1. Combine soy sauce, lime juice, honey, garlic, ginger, sesame oil and pepper flakes in small bowl. Combine cucumber, carrot, bell pepper and green onion in medium bowl. Stir 1 tablespoon soy sauce mixture into vegetable mixture.

2. Place about 1 tablespoon vegetable mixture on each lettuce leaf. Roll up leaves; top with sesame seeds just before serving. Serve with remaining sauce. *Makes 6 to 9 servings*

Curried Vegetable-Rice
Soup (p. 26)

Portobello & Fontina
Sandwiches (p. 52)

Sesame Rice Salad
(p. 38)

Chickpea Burgers
(p. 36)

Soups, Salads &
Sandwiches

Curried Vegetable-Rice Soup

Prep and Cook Time: 16 minutes

1 package (16 ounces) frozen Asian-blend vegetable medley, such as broccoli, cauliflower, sugar snap peas and red bell peppers
1 can (about 14 ounces) vegetable broth
¾ cup uncooked instant brown rice
2 teaspoons curry powder
½ teaspoon salt
½ teaspoon hot pepper sauce
1 can (14 ounces) unsweetened coconut milk
1 tablespoon fresh lime juice

1. Combine vegetables and broth in large saucepan. Cover; bring to a boil over high heat. Stir in rice, curry powder, salt and pepper sauce; reduce heat to medium-low. Cover and simmer 8 minutes or until rice is tender, stirring once.

2. Stir in coconut milk; cook 3 minutes or until heated through. Remove from heat. Stir in lime juice. Serve immediately.   *Makes 4 servings*

Variation: For a lighter soup with less fat and fewer calories, substitute light unsweetened coconut milk. Most large supermarkets carry this in their international foods section.

Spicy Orzo and Black Bean Salad

Prep and Cook Time: 25 minutes

2 tablespoons olive oil
2 tablespoons minced jalapeño pepper,* divided
1 teaspoon chili powder
6 cups water
¾ cup uncooked orzo pasta
1 cup frozen mixed vegetables
1 can (about 15 ounces) black beans, rinsed and drained
2 thin slices red onion, separated into rings
¼ cup chopped fresh cilantro
¼ cup fresh lime juice
¼ cup fresh lemon juice
4 cups washed and torn spinach leaves
2 tablespoons crumbled blue cheese

*Jalapeño peppers can sting and irritate the skin, so wear rubber gloves when handling peppers and do not touch your eyes.

1. Combine oil, 1 tablespoon jalapeño and chili powder in medium bowl; set aside.

2. Bring water and remaining 1 tablespoon jalapeño to a boil in large saucepan. Add orzo. Cook 10 to 12 minutes or until tender; drain. Rinse under cold water; drain.

3. Place frozen vegetables in small microwavable dish. Cover and microwave on HIGH 3 minutes or until hot. Let stand 5 minutes.

4. Add orzo, vegetables, black beans, onion, cilantro, lime juice and lemon juice to olive oil mixture; toss to coat. Divide spinach evenly among serving plates. Top with orzo mixture. Sprinkle with blue cheese.

Makes 4 servings

Barbecued Tofu Sandwiches

1 package (14 ounces) extra firm tofu
1 bottle (18 ounces) barbecue sauce
4 to 6 pieces frozen Texas toast, prepared according to package directions
Coleslaw

1. Place tofu on paper-towel lined plate; cover with another paper towel. Place weighted saucepan or baking dish on top of tofu. Let stand 15 minutes to drain. Cut tofu into 8 equal slices.

2. Spread half of barbecue sauce in large saucepan; arrange tofu slices over sauce in single layer. Cover with remaining sauce. Cover; cook over medium heat about 10 minutes or until tofu is hot, carefully turning tofu after 5 minutes.

3. Serve tofu on top of Texas toast. Drizzle with sauce; serve with coleslaw.

Makes 4 to 6 servings

Meatless Lentil Chili

½ cup USA lentils, rinsed
1 cup water
¼ packet (1 ounce) dry onion soup mix
½ cup tomato sauce
¼ teaspoon chili powder
⅛ teaspoon ground cumin

In a large saucepan, bring lentils and water to a boil. Add dry onion soup mix and simmer for 30 minutes. Add the rest of the ingredients and simmer 30 minutes longer. Serve over spaghetti, rice, or corn chips. Garnish with cheese. Chili can also be used on pizza, in tacos, or as a dip.

Makes 1 serving

Favorite recipe from **USA Dry Pea & Lentil Council**

Hearty Vegetable Soup

1 tablespoon olive oil
1 cup chopped onion
¾ cup chopped carrots
3 cloves garlic, minced
4 cups coarsely chopped green cabbage
3½ cups coarsely chopped red potatoes (about 3 medium)
1 teaspoon dried rosemary
1 teaspoon salt
½ teaspoon black pepper
4 cups vegetable broth
1 can (15 ounces) Great Northern beans, rinsed and drained
1 can (about 14 ounces) diced tomatoes
Grated Parmesan cheese (optional)

1. Heat oil in large saucepan over high heat. Add onion and carrots; cook and stir 3 minutes. Add garlic; cook and stir 1 minute.

2. Add cabbage, potatoes, rosemary, salt and pepper; cook 1 minute. Stir in broth, beans and tomatoes; bring to a boil. Reduce heat to medium-low; simmer about 15 minutes or until potatoes are tender. Serve with cheese. *Makes 6 to 8 servings*

Very Verde Green Bean Salad

Prep Time: 5 minutes • **Start to Finish:** 15 minutes

1 tablespoon olive oil
1 pound fresh green beans
½ cup water
½ teaspoon salt
½ teaspoon black pepper
½ cup ORTEGA® Salsa Verde
2 tablespoons ORTEGA® Garden Vegetable Salsa

Heat oil in large skillet over medium heat. When oil begins to shimmer, add green beans; toss lightly in oil. Heat about 3 minutes, tossing to coat beans well.

Add water, salt and pepper carefully. Cover; cook 5 minutes or until beans are tender. Add salsas; toss to coat beans evenly. Heat 1 or 2 minutes to warm salsas. Refrigerate or serve at room temperature.

Makes 4 servings

Crunchy Fruit Salad

Prep Time: 10 minutes

3 cups mixed salad greens
1 (11-ounce) can mandarin oranges, drained
½ cup fresh blueberries
20 sprays WISH-BONE® SALAD SPRITZERS® BALSAMIC BREEZE®
  Vinaigrette Dressing
½ cup nutty granola cereal mix

On serving platter, arrange salad greens, then top with oranges and blueberries. Spritz with WISH-BONE® SALAD SPRITZERS® BALSAMIC BREEZE® Vinaigrette Dressing, then sprinkle with granola.

Makes 2 servings

Chickpea Burgers

1 can (15 ounces) chickpeas, rinsed and drained
⅓ cup chopped carrots
⅓ cup herbed croutons
¼ cup chopped fresh parsley
¼ cup chopped onion
1 egg white
1 teaspoon minced garlic
1 teaspoon grated lemon peel
½ teaspoon black pepper
⅛ teaspoon salt
   Nonstick cooking spray
4 whole grain hamburger buns
   Tomato slices, lettuce leaves and salsa (optional)

1. Place chickpeas, carrots, croutons, parsley, onion, egg white, garlic, lemon peel, pepper and salt in food processor; process until blended. Shape mixture into 4 patties.

2. Spray 12-inch nonstick skillet with cooking spray; heat over medium heat. Add patties; cook 4 to 5 minutes or until bottoms are browned. Spray tops of patties with cooking spray; turn and cook 4 to 5 minutes or until browned.

3. Serve patties on buns with tomato, lettuce and salsa.

Makes 4 servings

Chickpea Burger

Sesame Rice Salad

1 can (15 ounces) mandarin orange segments, undrained
1 teaspoon ground ginger
2 cups MINUTE® Brown Rice, uncooked
½ cup Asian sesame salad dressing
3 green onions, thinly sliced
1 can (8 ounces) sliced water chestnuts, drained and chopped
½ cup sliced celery

Drain oranges, reserving liquid. Add enough water to reserved liquid to measure 1¾ cups. Stir in ginger. Prepare rice according to package directions, substituting 1¾ cups orange liquid for water. Refrigerate cooked rice 30 minutes. Add dressing, onions, water chestnuts and celery; mix lightly. Gently stir in oranges.   *Makes 4 servings*

Pear & Gorgonzola Melts

4 ounces creamy Gorgonzola cheese (do not use crumbled blue cheese)
8 slices walnut raisin bread
2 pears, cored and sliced
½ cup fresh spinach leaves
Melted butter

1. Spread cheese evenly on 4 bread slices; layer with pears and spinach. Top with remaining bread slices. Brush outsides of sandwiches with butter.

2. Place large nonstick skillet over medium heat until hot. Add sandwiches; cook 4 to 5 minutes per side or until cheese melts and sandwiches are golden brown.   *Makes 4 sandwiches*

Kohlrabi and Carrot Slaw

2 pounds kohlrabi bulbs, peeled and shredded
2 medium carrots, shredded
1 small red bell pepper, chopped
8 cherry tomatoes, cut into halves
2 green onions, thinly sliced
¼ cup mayonnaise
¼ cup plain yogurt
2 tablespoons cider vinegar
2 tablespoons finely chopped fresh parsley
1 teaspoon dried dill weed
¼ teaspoon salt
¼ teaspoon ground cumin
⅛ teaspoon black pepper

1. Combine kohlrabi, carrots, bell pepper, tomatoes and green onions in medium bowl.

2. Combine mayonnaise, yogurt, vinegar, parsley, dill, salt, cumin and black pepper in small bowl until smooth. Add to vegetables; toss to coat. Cover; refrigerate until ready to serve. *Makes 8 servings*

*Tip

Kohlrabi, like broccoli, cabbage, brussels sprouts, kale and cauliflower, is a member of the Brassica oleracea family. Kohlrabi has long been popular in Europe but never caught on much in the United States. Select small kohlrabi as they will be tastier and have better texture than larger ones.

Brazilian Black Bean Soup

Prep Time: 10 minutes • **Cook Time:** 30 minutes

1 red onion, chopped
2 cloves garlic, minced
1 can (29 ounces) black beans, drained
1 can (14½ ounces) vegetable broth
3 tablespoons *Frank's® RedHot®* Original Cayenne
Pepper Sauce
2 tablespoons chopped cilantro
2 teaspoons ground cumin
2 tablespoons rum or sherry (optional)

1. Heat *1 tablespoon oil* in 3-quart saucepot. Cook and stir onion and garlic 3 minutes or just until tender. Stir in *1½ cups water* and remaining ingredients *except* rum. Heat to boiling. Reduce heat to medium-low. Cook, partially covered, 20 minutes or until flavors are blended, stirring occasionally.

2. Ladle about half of soup into blender or food processor. Cover securely. Process on low speed until mixture is smooth. Return to saucepot. Stir in rum. Cook over medium-low heat 3 minutes or until heated through and flavors are blended. Garnish with lime slices, sour cream, minced onion or cilantro, if desired.   *Makes 4 to 6 servings*

Roasted Vegetable Salad

1 cup sliced mushrooms
1 cup sliced carrots
1 cup chopped green or yellow bell pepper
1 cup cherry tomatoes, halved
½ cup chopped onion
2 tablespoons chopped pitted kalamata olives
2 teaspoons lemon juice, divided
2 teaspoons olive oil
1 teaspoon dried oregano
½ teaspoon black pepper
1 teaspoon sugar
3 cups packed torn stemmed spinach or baby spinach

1. Preheat oven to 375°F. Combine mushrooms, carrots, bell pepper, tomatoes, onion, olives, 1 teaspoon lemon juice, oil, oregano and black pepper in large bowl; toss until evenly coated.

2. Spread vegetables in single layer on baking sheet. Bake 20 minutes, stirring once during baking. Stir in remaining 1 teaspoon lemon juice and sugar. Serve warm over spinach. *Makes 2 servings*

*Tip

As long as you're roasting vegetables, make extra for another meal. Toss the extra vegetables with olive oil or marinara sauce and serve over pasta. Or, stir the vegetables into brown rice or risotto. Roasted vegetables are also a great filling for vegetarian sandwiches. Spread pesto or garlic mayonnaise on French or whole grain bread, top with vegetables and a piece of cheese and broil until melted.

Waldorf Brown Rice Salad

2 medium Golden Delicious or Cortland apples
1 tablespoon lemon juice
2 cups cooked SUCCESS®, MAHATMA®, CAROLINA® or RICELAND® Whole Grain Brown Rice, cooled
½ cup chopped celery
½ cup chopped walnuts
½ cup raisins or sweetened dried cranberries
½ cup fat-free mayonnaise
¾ cup nonfat vanilla yogurt
   Spring salad greens (optional)

Wash, core and dice apples, without peeling. Place apples in large bowl and toss with lemon juice. Add rice, celery, nuts and raisins; toss to combine. In medium bowl, combine mayonnaise and yogurt. Blend well. Fold into rice mixture. Serve over salad greens, if desired.

Makes 4 servings

Havarti & Onion Sandwiches

1½ teaspoons olive oil
⅓ cup thinly sliced red onion
4 slices pumpernickel bread
6 ounces dill havarti cheese, cut into slices
½ cup prepared coleslaw

1. Heat oil in large skillet over medium heat. Add onion; cook and stir 5 minutes or until tender. Layer 2 bread slices with onion, cheese and coleslaw; top with remaining 2 bread slices.

2. Heat same skillet over medium heat. Add sandwiches; press down with spatula or weigh down with small plate. Cook 4 to 5 minutes on each side or until cheese melts and sandwiches are browned.

Makes 2 sandwiches

Two-Cheese Potato and Cauliflower Soup

1 tablespoon butter
1 cup chopped onion
2 cloves garlic, minced
5 cups whole milk
1 pound Yukon gold potatoes, diced
1 pound cauliflower florets
1½ teaspoons salt
⅛ teaspoon ground red pepper
1½ cups (6 ounces) shredded sharp Cheddar cheese
⅓ cup crumbled blue cheese

1. Melt butter in saucepan over medium-high heat. Add onion; cook and stir 4 minutes or until translucent. Add garlic; cook and stir 15 seconds. Add milk, potatoes, cauliflower, salt and red pepper; bring to a boil. Reduce heat; cover tightly and simmer 15 minutes or until potatoes are tender. Cool slightly.

2. Working in batches, process soup in blender or food processor until smooth. Return to saucepan. Heat 2 to 3 minutes over medium heat or until heated through. Remove from heat; add cheeses. Stir until melted.

Makes 4 to 6 servings

Big Easy Chili

3 cans (about 14 ounces each) New Orleans-style red beans
3 cans (about 14 ounces each) black-eyed peas, drained
1 can (28 ounces) diced tomatoes with green pepper and onion
Corn bread or buttermilk biscuits

1. Combine red beans, black-eyed peas and tomatoes in large saucepan or Dutch oven. Cook and stir over medium heat until heated through, stirring occasionally.

2. Serve with corn bread.

Makes 6 servings

Ravioli Panzanella Salad

1 package (9 ounces) refrigerated fresh cheese ravioli or tortellini
2 tablespoons olive oil
2 teaspoons white wine vinegar
⅛ teaspoon black pepper
1 cup halved grape tomatoes *or* 1 large tomato, chopped
½ cup sliced pimiento-stuffed olives
¼ cup finely chopped celery
1 large shallot, finely chopped *or* ¼ cup finely chopped red onion
¼ cup finely chopped Italian parsley

1. Cook ravioli according to package directions; drain well. Transfer to large serving bowl; set aside to cool 10 minutes.

2. Whisk oil, vinegar and black pepper in small bowl until well blended. Add to ravioli with tomatoes, olives, celery and shallot; toss gently. Sprinkle with parsley. *Makes 4 to 6 servings*

Green Chile Tomato Soup

Prep Time: 3 minutes • **Start to Finish:** 8 minutes

1 can (10.75 ounces) condensed tomato soup, undiluted
¾ cup milk
1 can (4 ounces) ORTEGA® Diced Green Chiles
½ cup (2 ounces) shredded Cheddar cheese

Combine soup, milk and chiles in small saucepan until blended. Cook and stir over medium heat until heated through. Sprinkle with cheese before serving. *Makes 2 servings*

Portobello & Fontina Sandwiches

2 teaspoons olive oil
2 large portobello mushrooms, stems removed
  Salt and black pepper
2 to 3 tablespoons sun-dried tomato pesto
4 slices crusty Italian bread
4 ounces fontina cheese, sliced
½ cup fresh basil leaves
  Additional olive oil

1. Preheat broiler. Line baking sheet with foil.

2. Drizzle 2 teaspoons oil over both sides of mushrooms; season with salt and pepper. Place mushrooms, gill sides up, on prepared baking sheet. Broil mushrooms 4 minutes per side or until tender. Cut into ¼-inch-thick slices.

3. Spread pesto evenly on 2 bread slices; layer with mushrooms, cheese and basil. Top with remaining bread slices. Brush outsides of sandwiches lightly with additional oil.

4. Heat large grill pan or skillet over medium heat. Add sandwiches; press down lightly with spatula or weigh down with small plate. Cook sandwiches 4 to 5 minutes per side or until cheese melts and sandwiches are golden brown. *Makes 2 sandwiches*

Mediterranean Main Salad

1⅓ cups water
⅔ cup uncooked quick-cooking pearl barley
1 can (14 ounces) quartered artichoke hearts, drained and coarsely chopped
2 medium tomatoes, seeded and chopped
¼ cup chopped parsley
1 tablespoon dried Greek seasoning
1 teaspoon grated lemon peel
2 tablespoons lemon juice
1 tablespoon extra-virgin olive oil
1 package (4 ounces) feta cheese, crumbled

1. Bring water a to boil in medium saucepan. Stir in barley. Reduce heat; cover and simmer 10 to 12 minutes or until tender.

2. Meanwhile, combine artichokes, tomatoes, parsley, seasoning, lemon peel, lemon juice and oil in large bowl. Toss gently to blend.

3. Drain barley. Rinse with cold water to cool quickly; drain well.

4. Add barley to artichoke mixture; toss well. Add cheese; toss gently to blend. *Makes 4 servings*

Grilled 3-Cheese Sandwiches

2 slices (1 ounce each) Muenster cheese
2 slices (1 ounce each) Swiss cheese
2 slices (1 ounce each) Cheddar cheese
2 teaspoons Dijon mustard or Dijon mustard mayonnaise
4 slices sourdough bread
   Melted butter

1. Place 1 slice of each cheese on 2 bread slices. Spread mustard over cheese; top with remaining bread slices. Brush outsides of sandwiches with butter.

2. Place large nonstick skillet over medium heat until hot. Add sandwiches; press down lightly with spatula or weigh down with small plate. Cook sandwiches 4 to 5 minutes per side or until cheese melts and sandwiches are golden brown. *Makes 2 sandwiches*

Summer's Best Gazpacho

3 cups tomato juice
2½ cups finely diced tomatoes (2 large)
1 cup finely diced yellow or red bell pepper (1 small)
1 cup finely diced unpeeled cucumber
½ cup chunky salsa
1 tablespoon olive oil
1 clove garlic, minced
1 ripe avocado, diced
¼ cup finely chopped cilantro or basil

1. Combine tomato juice, tomatoes, bell pepper, cucumber, salsa, oil and garlic in large bowl. Mix well.

2. Cover. Chill at least 1 hour or up to 24 hours before serving. Stir in avocado and cilantro just before serving. *Makes 6 servings*

Grilled Zucchini with Pine
Nuts & Goat Cheese (p. 62)

Sweet-Sour Cabbage with App
and Caraway Seeds (p. 68)

Seitan Fajitas
(p. 60)

Glazed Parsnips and
Carrots (p. 70)

Fabulous Vegetables

Seitan Fajitas

1 packet (1 ounce) fajita seasoning
2 packages (8 ounces each) seitan,* sliced
1 tablespoon vegetable oil
1 red bell pepper, sliced
½ medium onion, sliced
1 package (8 ounces) sliced mushrooms
6 (6- to 7-inch) tortillas, warmed
Salsa and sour cream (optional)

*Seitan is a meat substitute made from wheat gluten. It is high in protein and has a meaty, chewy texture. It can be found in the refrigerated section of large supermarkets and specialty food stores.

1. Dissolve seasoning according to package directions. Place seitan in large resealable food storage bag. Pour seasoning mixture over seitan. Seal bag; shake to coat.

2. Heat oil in large skillet. Add pepper and onion; cook and stir 4 to 5 minutes or until crisp-tender. Add mushrooms; cook and stir 1 to 2 minutes or until mushrooms are softened. Add seitan and seasoning mixture; cook and stir 1 to 2 minutes or until seitan is heated through and vegetables are coated with seasoning.

3. Divide vegetable mixture evenly among tortillas. Serve with salsa and sour cream, if desired. *Makes 6 fajitas*

Grilled Zucchini With Pine Nuts & Goat Cheese

Prep Time: 5 minutes • **Marinate Time:** 30 minutes
Cook Time: 6 minutes

½ cup LAWRY'S® Lemon Pepper Marinade With Lemon Juice
2 pounds zucchini, halved lengthwise
½ cup pine nuts, toasted
½ cup crumbled goat cheese

1. In large resealable plastic bag, pour ¼ cup LAWRY'S® Lemon Pepper Marinade With Lemon Juice over zucchini; turn to coat. Close bag and marinate in refrigerator 30 minutes.

2. Remove zucchini from Marinade, discarding Marinade. Grill or broil zucchini, turning once and brushing frequently with remaining ¼ cup Marinade, 6 minutes or until tender; coarsely chop.

3. Toss zucchini with pine nuts, then top with cheese.

Makes 4 servings

Note: Also terrific with LAWRY'S® Herb & Garlic Marinade With Lemon Juice or LAWRY'S® Italian Garlic Steak Marinade With Roasted Garlic & Olive Oil.

Mexican-Style Corn on the Cob

2 tablespoons mayonnaise
½ teaspoon chili powder
½ teaspoon grated lime peel
4 ears corn, shucked
2 tablespoons grated Parmesan cheese

1. Heat grill to medium-high. Combine mayonnaise, chili powder and lime peel in small bowl; set aside.

2. Grill corn 4 to 6 minutes or until lightly charred, turning 3 times. Immediately spread mayonnaise mixture over corn. Sprinkle with cheese.

Makes 4 servings

Southwest Spaghetti Squash

1 spaghetti squash (about 3 pounds)
1 can (about 14 ounces) Mexican-style diced tomatoes
1 can (about 14 ounces) black beans, rinsed and drained
¾ cup (3 ounces) shredded Monterey Jack cheese, divided
¼ cup finely chopped cilantro
1 teaspoon ground cumin
¼ teaspoon garlic salt
¼ teaspoon black pepper

1. Preheat oven to 350°F. Spray baking pan and 1½-quart baking dish with nonstick cooking spray.

2. Cut squash in half lengthwise. Remove and discard seeds. Place squash, cut side down, in prepared baking pan. Bake 45 minutes to 1 hour or just until tender. Shred hot squash with fork; place in large bowl. (Use oven mitts to protect hands.)

3. Add tomatoes, beans, ½ cup cheese, cilantro, cumin, garlic salt and pepper; toss well. Spoon mixture into prepared dish. Sprinkle with remaining ¼ cup cheese.

4. Bake, uncovered, 30 to 35 minutes or until heated through. Serve immediately. *Makes 4 servings*

Mongolian Vegetables

1 package (about 14 ounces) firm tofu, drained
4 tablespoons soy sauce, divided
1 tablespoon dark sesame oil
1 large head bok choy (about 1½ pounds)
2 teaspoons cornstarch
1 tablespoon peanut or vegetable oil
1 red or yellow bell pepper, cut into short thin strips
2 cloves garlic, minced
4 green onions, cut into ½-inch pieces
2 teaspoons sesame seeds, toasted*

To toast sesame seeds, spread seeds in small skillet. Shake skillet over medium-low heat 3 minutes or until seeds begin to pop and turn golden.

1. Press tofu lightly between paper towels; cut into ¾-inch squares or triangles. Place in shallow dish. Combine 2 tablespoons soy sauce and sesame oil; drizzle over tofu. Let stand while preparing vegetables.

2. Cut stems from bok choy leaves; slice stems into ½-inch pieces. Cut leaves crosswise into ½-inch slices.

3. Blend remaining 2 tablespoons soy sauce into cornstarch in small bowl until smooth.

4. Heat peanut oil in wok or large skillet over medium-high heat. Add bok choy stems, bell pepper and garlic; stir-fry 5 minutes. Add bok choy leaves and green onions; stir-fry 2 minutes.

5. Stir soy sauce mixture and add to wok along with tofu mixture. Stir-fry 30 seconds or until sauce boils and thickens. Sprinkle with sesame seeds.

Makes 2 to 4 servings

Sweet-Sour Cabbage with Apples and Caraway Seeds

4 cups shredded red cabbage
1 large tart apple, peeled, cored and cut into ¼-inch-thick slices
¼ cup packed light brown sugar
¼ cup water
¼ cup cider vinegar
½ teaspoon salt
¼ teaspoon caraway seeds
   Dash black pepper

1. Combine all ingredients in large saucepan. Cook, covered, over medium heat 10 minutes; stir.

2. Cook, covered, over medium-low heat 15 to 20 minutes or until cabbage is crisp-tender and apple is tender. Serve warm or chilled.

Makes 6 servings

Lemon-Scented Broccoli with Golden Shallots

1½ pounds fresh broccoli
1 tablespoon olive oil
½ cup thinly sliced shallots or red onion
1 teaspoon finely shredded lemon peel
⅛ teaspoon black pepper
¼ teaspoon salt

1. Cut broccoli into florets. Thinly slice 1 cup stems. Place in microwavable casserole. Add 2 tablespoons water. Cover and microwave on HIGH 4 to 5 minutes or until crisp-tender. Drain.

2. Meanwhile, heat oil in small skillet over medium heat. Add shallots. Cook and stir 5 minutes or until golden.

3. Add shallots, lemon peel, pepper and salt to broccoli. Toss lightly.

Makes 4 servings

Glazed Parsnips and Carrots

1 pound parsnips (2 large or 3 medium)
1 bag (8 ounces) baby carrots
1 tablespoon oil
   Salt and black pepper
¼ cup orange juice
1 tablespoon butter
1 tablespoon honey
⅛ teaspoon ground ginger

1. Preheat oven to 425°F. Peel parsnips; cut into wedges the same size as baby carrots.

2. Spread vegetables in shallow roasting pan. Drizzle with oil and sprinkle with salt and pepper; toss to coat. Bake 30 to 35 minutes or until fork-tender.

3. Combine orange juice, butter, honey and ginger in large skillet. Add roasted vegetables; cook and stir over high heat 1 to 2 minutes, stirring frequently, until sauce thickens and coats vegetables. Season with additional salt and pepper.   *Makes 6 servings*

*Tip

Parsnips are used in many of the same ways as carrots and often they are served together. Their sweetness is enhanced by brown sugar, apples, orange peel and spices like cinnamon, ginger or nutmeg. Parsnips also pair well with savory herbs such as rosemary, chives and thyme. Try adding parsnips to soups, stews and other vegetable dishes.

Grilled Eggplant Parmesan

Prep Time: 15 minutes • **Marinate Time:** 15 minutes
Cook Time: 15 minutes

¾ cup LAWRY'S® Italian Garlic Steak Marinade With Roasted Garlic & Olive Oil
1 medium eggplant, cut into ½-inch thick slices
1 medium tomato, sliced
1½ cups shredded fresh mozzarella cheese (about 6 ounces)
¼ teaspoon LAWRY'S® Seasoned Pepper
¼ cup fresh basil leaves (optional)

1. In large resealable plastic bag, pour ½ cup LAWRY'S® Italian Garlic Steak Marinade With Roasted Garlic & Olive Oil over eggplant; turn to coat. Close bag and marinate 15 minutes.

2. Remove eggplant from Marinade. Grill, turning once and brushing with remaining ¼ cup Marinade, 10 minutes or until tender.

3. Top grilled eggplant with tomato, mozzarella and LAWRY'S® Seasoned Pepper. Grill 2 minutes or until cheese is melted. Garnish with basil, if desired.   *Makes 4 servings*

Tip: Serve on a grilled hamburger bun for an easy and quick sandwich.

Variation: Also terrific with LAWRY'S® Herb & Garlic Marinade With Lemon Juice.

Veggie-Stuffed Portobello Mushrooms

4 large portobello mushrooms (about 1¼ to 1½ pounds)
    Nonstick cooking spray
2 teaspoons olive oil or butter
1 cup chopped green or red bell pepper
⅓ cup sliced shallots or chopped onion
2 cloves garlic, minced
1 cup chopped zucchini or summer squash
½ teaspoon salt
¼ teaspoon black pepper
1 cup panko bread crumbs* or toasted fresh bread crumbs
1 cup (4 ounces) shredded sharp Cheddar or mozzarella
    cheese

Panko bread crumbs are used in Japanese cooking to provide a crisp exterior to fried foods. They are coarser than ordinary bread crumbs.

1. Preheat broiler. Line baking sheet with foil. Gently remove mushroom stems; chop and set aside. Scrape off and discard brown gills from mushroom caps using spoon. Place mushrooms, cap side up, on prepared baking sheet. Coat tops lightly with cooking spray. Broil 4 to 5 inches from heat 5 minutes or until tender.

2. Meanwhile, heat oil in large nonstick skillet over medium-high heat. Add bell pepper, shallots and garlic; cook and stir 5 minutes or until bell peppers begin to brown on edges. Stir in zucchini, chopped mushroom stems, salt and black pepper; cook and stir 3 to 4 minutes or until vegetables are tender. Remove from heat; cool 5 minutes. Stir in bread crumbs and cheese.

3. Turn mushroom caps over. Mound vegetable mixture into caps. Broil 2 to 3 minutes or until golden brown and cheese is melted.

Makes 4 servings

Thyme-Scented Roasted Sweet Potatoes and Onions

2 large unpeeled sweet potatoes (about 1¼ pounds)
1 medium sweet or yellow onion, cut into chunks
2 tablespoons oil
1 teaspoon dried thyme
½ teaspoon salt
½ teaspoon paprika (preferably smoked)
⅛ teaspoon ground red pepper

1. Preheat oven to 425°F. Coat 15×10-inch jelly roll pan with nonstick cooking spray.

2. Cut sweet potatoes into 1-inch chunks. Combine potatoes and onion in large bowl. Add oil, thyme, salt, paprika and red pepper; toss well. Spread vegetables in single layer on prepared pan.

3. Bake 20 to 25 minutes or until very tender, stirring after 10 minutes. Let stand 5 minutes before serving.   *Makes 4 to 6 servings*

Zucchini Romano

Prep Time: 10 minutes • **Cook Time:** 7 minutes

5 medium zucchini or yellow squash, sliced ¼-inch thick
1⅓ cups *French's*® Cheddar or Original French Fried Onions
⅔ cup shredded Parmesan cheese
⅛ teaspoon ground nutmeg
2 tablespoons melted butter

1. Boil zucchini for 5 minutes until just tender. Drain well.

2. Heat French Fried Onions on a microwave-safe plate in microwave for 45 seconds.

3. Mix French Fried Onions, cheese and nutmeg in plastic bag. Crush onions with hands or rolling pin.

4. Layer ⅓ of the zucchini with ⅓ of the onion mixture in serving bowl. Drizzle with ⅓ of the butter. Repeat layers twice.   *Makes 6 servings*

Tuscan Kalamata Olive and White Bean Pasta (p. 90)

Tofu Rigatoni Casserole (p. 80)

Zucchini Mushroom Lasagna with Tofu (p. 82)

Spaghetti with Pesto Tofu Squares (p. 88)

Simple **Pastas**

Tofu Rigatoni Casserole

½ (16-ounce) package uncooked rigatoni (3 cups)
4 cups loosely packed baby spinach
1 cup soft tofu
1 egg
¼ teaspoon salt
¼ teaspoon black pepper
¼ teaspoon ground nutmeg (optional)
1 can (about 14 ounces) diced tomatoes with basil, garlic and oregano
1 can (about 14 ounces) quartered artichokes, drained and chopped
2 cups (8 ounces) shredded Italian cheese blend, divided

1. Preheat oven to 350°F. Spray 11×7-inch baking dish with nonstick cooking spray.

2. Cook rigatoni in large saucepan according to package directions. Stir in spinach in bunches during last 2 minutes of cooking. Drain; return to saucepan.

3. Meanwhile, combine tofu, egg, salt, pepper and nutmeg, if desired, in medium bowl; mix until blended. Fold tofu mixture into rigatoni. Add tomatoes, artichokes and 1½ cups cheese; mix well. Spoon into prepared baking dish.

4. Bake 20 minutes or until bubbly. Top with remaining ½ cup cheese. Bake 10 minutes or until cheese is browned.   *Makes 6 servings*

Note: If the saucepan is too small to cook the spinach with the pasta, chop the spinach and stir in with the tomatoes.

Zucchini and Mushroom Lasagna with Tofu

1 tablespoon olive oil
1 cup chopped onions
1 package (8 ounces) sliced mushrooms
2 small zucchini, thinly sliced
½ teaspoon black pepper, divided
½ (14-ounce) package soft or firm tofu
1 egg
¼ teaspoon salt
1 jar (26 ounces) spicy red pepper pasta sauce
9 uncooked no-boil lasagna noodles
2 cups (8 ounces) shredded Italian cheese blend
¼ cup shredded Parmesan cheese

1. Preheat oven to 350°F. Spray 9-inch square baking dish with nonstick cooking spray.

2. Heat oil in large skillet. Add onions; cook and stir 2 minutes. Add mushrooms, zucchini and ¼ teaspoon pepper. Cook 8 minutes or until slightly cooked.

3. Meanwhile, combine tofu, egg, salt and remaining ¼ teaspoon pepper in medium bowl. Mix until smooth; set aside.

4. Spread ½ cup pasta sauce over bottom of prepared dish. Arrange 3 noodles over sauce. Layer one third each vegetable mixture, tofu mixture, pasta sauce and Italian cheese blend. Repeat layers twice. Cover with foil.

5. Bake 1 hour. Remove foil; sprinkle with Parmesan cheese. Bake, uncovered, 15 minutes or until cheese is browned. Let stand 15 minutes before serving.   *Makes 4 to 6 servings*

Baked Ravioli
with Pumpkin Sauce

1 package (9 ounces) refrigerated cheese ravioli
1 tablespoon butter
1 shallot, finely chopped
1 cup whipping cream
1 cup solid-pack pumpkin
½ cup shredded Asiago cheese, divided
½ teaspoon salt
¼ teaspoon ground nutmeg
⅛ teaspoon black pepper
½ cup small croutons or coarse bread crumbs

1. Preheat oven to 350°F. Grease 2-quart baking dish; set aside. Bring large pot of salted water to a boil. Cook ravioli according to package directions until tender; drain well.

2. Meanwhile, melt butter in medium saucepan. Add shallot; cook and stir over medium heat 3 minutes or until tender. Add cream, pumpkin, ¼ cup cheese, salt, nutmeg and pepper; cook and stir over low heat 2 minutes or until cheese melts. Gently stir in cooked ravioli.

3. Spoon ravioli and pumpkin sauce mixture into prepared baking dish. Combine remaining ¼ cup cheese and croutons; sprinkle over ravioli.

4. Bake 15 minutes or until sauce is heated through and topping is lightly browned. *Makes 4 servings*

Soba
Stir-Fry

8 ounces uncooked soba (buckwheat) noodles
1 tablespoon olive oil
2 cups sliced shiitake mushrooms
1 medium red bell pepper, cut into thin strips
2 whole dried red chiles *or* **¼ teaspoon red pepper flakes**
1 clove garlic, minced
2 cups shredded napa cabbage
½ cup vegetable broth
2 tablespoons tamari or soy sauce
1 tablespoon rice wine or dry sherry
2 teaspoons cornstarch
1 package (14 ounces) firm tofu, drained and cut into
1-inch cubes
2 green onions, thinly sliced

1. Cook noodles according to package directions. Drain and set aside.

2. Heat oil in large nonstick skillet or wok over medium heat. Add mushrooms, bell pepper, dried chiles and garlic. Cook and stir 3 minutes or until mushrooms are tender. Add cabbage. Cover; cook 2 minutes or until cabbage is wilted.

3. Combine broth, tamari, rice wine and cornstarch in small bowl. Stir sauce into vegetable mixture. Cook 2 minutes or until sauce is thickened.

4. Stir in tofu and noodles; toss gently until heated through. Sprinkle with green onions. Serve immediately. *Makes 4 servings*

Spaghetti with Pesto Tofu Squares

½ (16-ounce) package uncooked spaghetti
1 jar (24 ounces) marinara sauce
1 package (14 ounces) extra firm tofu
¼ to ½ cup pesto
½ cup shredded Parmesan cheese
¼ cup pine nuts, toasted*

To toast nuts, spread in shallow baking pan. Bake in preheated 350°F oven 5 to 10 minutes or until golden, stirring frequently.

1. Preheat oven to 350°F. Spray shallow baking dish with nonstick cooking spray.

2. Cut tofu into 1-inch cubes. Toss with pesto in medium bowl. Arrange in prepared baking dish. Bake 15 minutes.

3. Meanwhile, cook spaghetti according to package directions. Drain; return to saucepan. Add marinara sauce; toss to coat. Cover; cook 5 minutes over low heat or until hot.

4. Divide spaghetti among 4 plates; top each serving evenly with tofu cubes. Sprinkle with cheese and pine nuts. *Makes 4 servings*

Tuscan Kalamata Olive and White Bean Pasta

2 tablespoons extra-virgin olive oil
1 clove garlic, minced
½ teaspoon salt
⅛ teaspoon red pepper flakes
6 ounces uncooked rotini pasta
1 can (about 15 ounces) navy beans
1 can (about 14 ounces) diced tomatoes
½ cup pitted kalamata olives
½ cup packed spinach leaves
¼ cup (1 ounce) pine nuts, toasted*
2 tablespoons chopped fresh basil
2 ounces crumbled feta with peppercorns**

*To toast nuts, spread in shallow baking pan. Bake in preheated 350°F oven 5 to 10 minutes or until golden, stirring frequently.

**If feta with peppercorns is unavailable, use plain feta and season pasta mixture with ¼ teaspoon black pepper.

1. Combine oil, garlic, salt and pepper flakes in small bowl; set aside.

2. Cook pasta according to package directions. Meanwhile, drain beans and tomatoes in colander. Pour pasta and cooking water over beans and tomatoes. Drain well. Transfer to large bowl. Add garlic mixture, olives, spinach, nuts and basil. Toss gently to blend well. Top with feta.

Makes 4 servings

Rice Noodles with Broccoli and Tofu

1 package (14 ounces) firm or extra firm tofu
1 package (8 to 10 ounces) wide rice noodles
2 tablespoons peanut oil
3 medium shallots, sliced
6 cloves garlic, minced
1 jalapeño pepper,* minced
2 teaspoons minced fresh ginger
3 cups broccoli florets
3 tablespoons regular soy sauce
1 tablespoon sweet soy sauce (or substitute regular)
  Fresh basil leaves (optional)

*Jalapeño peppers can sting and irritate the skin, so wear rubber gloves when handling peppers and do not touch your eyes.

1. Cut tofu crosswise into 2 pieces, each about 1 inch thick. Place tofu on cutting board between layers of paper towels; put another cutting board on top to press moisture out of tofu. Place rice noodles in large bowl; cover with boiling water. Let soak 30 minutes or until soft.

2. Cut tofu into bite-sized squares and blot dry. Heat oil in large skillet or wok over medium-high heat. Add tofu to skillet; stir-fry about 5 minutes or until tofu is lightly browned on all sides. Remove from skillet.

3. Add shallots, jalapeño pepper, garlic and ginger to skillet. Stir-fry 2 to 3 minutes. Add broccoli; stir-fry 1 minute. Cover and cook 3 minutes or until broccoli is crisp-tender.

4. Drain noodles well; stir into skillet. Return tofu to skillet; add soy sauces; stir-fry about 8 minutes or until noodles are coated and flavors are blended. Adjust seasoning. Garnish with basil.   *Makes 4 to 6 servings*

Spaghetti with Roasted Pepper and Tomato Sauce

1½ tablespoons olive oil
1 medium red onion, finely chopped
1 clove garlic, minced
2 Roasted Red Peppers* (recipe follows), chopped
1 can (about 14 ounces) diced roasted tomatoes
½ teaspoon salt
¼ teaspoon crushed dried oregano
¼ teaspoon chipotle chile flakes** or red pepper flakes
⅛ teaspoon black pepper
8 ounces whole wheat spaghetti, cooked
½ cup grated Parmesan cheese

Or substitute 3 jarred roasted red peppers
**Chipotle chile flakes are available in the spice section of the supermarket.*

1. Heat oil in large skillet until hot. Add onion and garlic. Cook and stir over medium-high heat 2 to 5 minutes or until tender. Add roasted peppers; cook 2 minutes.

2. Add tomatoes, salt, oregano, chile flakes and black pepper. Reduce heat to low. Simmer 10 minutes. Serve over spaghetti; top each serving with 2 tablespoons cheese. *Makes 4 servings*

Roasted Red Peppers: Adjust broiler rack to about 4 inches from heat source. Preheat broiler. Cover broiler pan with foil. Place 2 red bell peppers on prepared pan. Broil 15 to 20 minutes or until blackened on all sides, turning peppers every 5 minutes with tongs. Place peppers in paper bag. Close bag; let stand 15 to 20 minutes to loosen skin. Cut peppers in half and remove cores. Peel off skin with paring knife, rinsing under cold water to remove seeds and loose skin.

Creamy Fettuccine with Asparagus & Lima Beans

8 ounces uncooked fettuccine
2 tablespoons butter
2 cups fresh asparagus pieces (about 1 inch long)
1 cup frozen lima beans, thawed
¼ teaspoon black pepper
½ cup vegetable broth
1 cup half-and-half or whipping cream
1 cup grated Parmesan cheese

1. Cook fettuccine according to package directions. Drain well; cover and keep warm.

2. Meanwhile, melt butter in large skillet over medium-high heat. Add asparagus, lima beans and ¼ teaspoon pepper; cook and stir 3 minutes. Add broth; simmer 3 minutes. Add half-and-half; simmer 3 to 4 minutes or until vegetables are tender.

3. Add vegetable mixture and cheese to fettuccine; toss well. Serve immediately. *Makes 4 servings*

*Tip
There are two distinct varieties of lima beans. Fordhooks are large, slightly plump pale green beans with a full flavor. Baby limas, which are a separate variety, are half the size of Fordhooks and less plump. Use either variety in this recipe. Or, try using fresh fava beans when they are available.

Barley and Pear-Stuffed
Acorn Squash (p. 100)

Thai Seitan Stir-Fry
(p. 110)

Quinoa-Stuffed Tomatoes
(p. 108)

Sesame Ginger-Glazed Tofu
with Rice (p. 114)

Versatile Grains

Barley and Pear-Stuffed Acorn Squash

3 small acorn or carnival squash
2 cups vegetable broth
¾ teaspoon salt, divided
1 cup uncooked quick-cooking barley
2 tablespoons butter
1 small onion, chopped
1 stalk celery, chopped
¼ teaspoon black pepper
1 large ripe pear, unpeeled, diced
½ cup chopped hazelnuts, toasted*
¼ cup maple syrup
½ teaspoon cinnamon

*To toast hazelnuts, spread in single layer on baking sheet. Bake in preheated 350°F oven 7 to 10 minutes or until golden, stirring occasionally.

1. Pierce each squash with knife tip in several places. Microwave on HIGH 12 to 14 minutes or until tender, turning once. *Do not overcook.* Let stand 5 minutes. Cut squash in half lengthwise; scoop out seeds. Arrange halves in large baking dish.

2. Meanwhile, bring broth and ½ teaspoon salt to boil in large saucepan over high heat. Stir in barley; reduce heat to low. Cover; simmer 12 minutes or until tender. Do not drain.

3. Preheat oven to 350°F.

4. Melt butter in large skillet over medium heat. Add onion, celery, remaining ¼ teaspoon salt and pepper; cook and stir 5 minutes. Add pear; cook 5 minutes. Stir in barley, hazelnuts, syrup and cinnamon.

5. Spoon barley mixture into squash. Cover with foil. Bake 15 to 20 minutes or until heated through. *Makes 6 servings*

Barley and Apple-Stuffed Squash: Substitute 1 apple for pear and walnuts for hazelnuts.

Note: Squash can be stuffed ahead of time. Prepare as directed in steps 1 through 5. Do not bake. Cool; tightly cover and refrigerate. To serve, bake at 350°F 25 to 30 minutes or until hot.

Garlic Cheddar Grits

2 tablespoons butter
2 cloves garlic, minced
4 cups (32 ounces) vegetable broth*
1 cup grits (not instant)
**2 cups (8 ounces) shredded sharp Cheddar cheese, plus
    more for topping**
2 eggs
¼ to ½ teaspoon salt
    Hot pepper sauce or ground red pepper

This amount of broth will produce creamy grits. For a firmer texture, reduce broth to 3½ cups.

1. Melt butter in large heavy saucepan over medium-high heat. Add garlic; cook and stir 30 seconds. Add broth; bring to a boil over high heat. Stir in grits; reduce heat. Cover and simmer 15 minutes, stirring twice.

2. Meanwhile, preheat oven to 375°F. Lightly grease 1½-quart round casserole or 9-inch deep-dish pie plate.

3. Remove grits from heat; stir in cheese until melted. Beat eggs in small bowl until thick and pale yellow. Stir 1 spoonful of grits mixture into eggs until well blended. Fold egg mixture into remaining grits mixture until evenly blended. Season to taste with salt and hot pepper sauce. Spoon grits mixture into prepared casserole.

4. Bake, uncovered, 40 to 45 minutes or until golden brown and center is set. Top with additional cheese, if desired.   *Makes 8 servings*

Fried Brown Rice with Asian Vegetables

1 cup water
½ teaspoon salt, divided
1 cup uncooked instant brown rice
2½ tablespoons canola or vegetable oil, divided
2 cups frozen Asian mixed vegetables (about 8 ounces)
1 clove garlic, minced
4 eggs
⅛ teaspoon black pepper
¼ cup minced green onions
2 to 3 teaspoons soy sauce

1. Bring water and ¼ teaspoon salt to a boil in small saucepan. Stir in rice; reduce heat to low. Cover and simmer 5 minutes. Remove from heat; let stand, covered, 5 minutes.

2. Heat 1 tablespoon oil in large nonstick skillet. Add rice. Cook and stir over medium-high heat 3 to 5 minutes. Transfer to large bowl; set aside. Add ½ tablespoon oil to skillet. Add vegetables and garlic. Cook and stir over high heat 3 to 5 minutes or until vegetables are hot and any liquid evaporates. Transfer to bowl; set aside.

3. Add remaining 1 tablespoon oil to skillet. Beat eggs, pepper and remaining ¼ teaspoon salt in small bowl. Pour into skillet. Gently scramble over medium heat. When eggs are just set, break up eggs. Add rice mixture and green onions to skillet; mix well. Sprinkle with soy sauce. *Makes 4 servings*

Couscous Primavera

1 shallot, minced *or* **¼ cup minced red onion**
**8 medium spears fresh asparagus, cooked and cut
     into 1-inch pieces**
1 cup frozen peas
1 cup halved grape tomatoes
⅛ teaspoon salt
⅛ teaspoon black pepper
½ cup uncooked whole wheat couscous
¼ cup grated Parmesan cheese

1. Coat large skillet with nonstick cooking spray. Add shallot. Cook over medium-high heat 3 minutes or until tender. Add asparagus and peas. Cook 2 minutes or until peas are heated through. Add tomatoes; cook 2 minutes. Add salt, pepper and ¾ cup water. Bring to a boil.

2. Stir in couscous; reduce heat to low. Cover and simmer 2 minutes or until liquid is absorbed. Fluff with fork. Stir in cheese.

Makes 2 servings

Taco Rice and Beans

Prep Time: 5 minutes • **Start to Finish:** 15 minutes

2 tablespoons olive oil
1 medium onion, diced
1 cup water
1 packet (1.25 ounces) ORTEGA® Taco Seasoning Mix
1 can (15 ounces) JOAN OF ARC® Black Beans, drained
2 cups cooked rice
¼ cup ORTEGA® Thick & Chunky Salsa

Heat oil in skillet over medium heat until hot. Add onion. Cook and stir 3 minutes. Add water and seasoning mix. Cook and stir until combined and slightly thickened. Stir in beans, rice and salsa. Cook 5 minutes longer or until heated through. *Makes 4 servings*

Quinoa-Stuffed Tomatoes

½ cup uncooked quinoa
3 cups water
½ teaspoon salt, divided
1 tablespoon olive oil
1 red bell pepper, chopped
⅓ cup chopped green onion
⅛ teaspoon dried thyme
⅛ teaspoon black pepper
1 tablespoon butter
8 plum tomatoes,* halved, seeded and hollowed out

*Or substitute 4 medium tomatoes.

1. Preheat oven to 325°F. Place quinoa in fine-mesh sieve. Rinse well under cold running water. Bring water and ¼ teaspoon salt to a boil in small saucepan. Stir in quinoa. Cover; reduce heat to low. Simmer 12 to 14 minutes or until quinoa is tender and plump. Drain well; set aside.

2. Heat oil in large skillet over medium-high heat until hot. Add bell pepper. Cook and stir 7 to 10 minutes or until tender. Stir in quinoa, green onion, remaining ¼ teaspoon salt, thyme and black pepper. Add butter; stir until melted. Remove from heat.

3. Arrange tomato halves in baking dish. Fill with quinoa mixture. Bake 15 to 20 minutes or until tomatoes are tender. *Makes 8 servings*

Thai Seitan Stir-Fry

1 package (8 ounces) seitan,* drained and thinly sliced
1 jalapeño pepper,** halved and seeded
3 cloves garlic
1 piece peeled fresh ginger (about 1 inch)
⅓ cup soy sauce
¼ cup packed brown sugar
¼ cup lime juice (1 lime)
½ teaspoon red pepper flakes
¼ teaspoon salt
3 tablespoons vegetable oil
1 medium onion, chopped (about 2 cups)
2 red bell peppers, quartered and thinly sliced (about 2 cups)
2 cups ready-to-use fresh broccoli florets
3 green onions, sliced diagonally
4 cups lightly packed baby spinach
¼ cup fresh basil strips (about 8 leaves)
3 cups hot cooked rice
¼ cup salted peanuts, chopped

*Seitan is a meat substitute made from wheat gluten. It is high in protein and has a meaty, chewy texture. It can be found in the refrigerated section of large supermarkets and specialty food stores.

**Jalapeño peppers can sting and irritate the skin so wear rubber gloves when handling and do not touch your eyes.

1. Place seitan slices in medium bowl. Combine jalapeño, garlic and ginger in food processor; process until finely chopped. Add soy sauce, brown sugar, lime juice, red pepper flakes and salt; process until blended. Pour mixture over seitan; toss to coat. Marinate at least 20 minutes.

2. Heat oil in wok or large skillet over high heat. Add onion, bell peppers and broccoli. Stir-fry 3 to 5 minutes. Add seitan, marinade and green onions. Bring to a boil; stir-fry 3 minutes or until vegetables are crisp-tender and seitan is hot. Add spinach in 2 additions, stirring until beginning to wilt after each addition.

3. Stir in basil just before serving. Serve over rice; sprinkle with peanuts.

Makes 4 to 6 servings

Pan-Fried Polenta with Fresh Tomato-Bean Salsa

2½ cups chopped plum tomatoes
1 cup canned white beans, rinsed and drained
¼ cup chopped fresh basil leaves
½ teaspoon salt
½ teaspoon black pepper
2 tablespoons olive oil, divided
1 package (16 ounces) prepared polenta, sliced into
   ¼-inch-thick rounds
¼ cup grated Parmesan cheese
   Additional chopped fresh basil leaves

1. Stir together tomatoes, beans, basil, salt and pepper. Let stand at room temperature 15 minutes to blend flavors.

2. Heat 1 tablespoon olive oil in medium nonstick skillet over medium-high heat. Add half of polenta slices to skillet; cook 4 minutes or until golden brown on both sides, turning once. Remove polenta from skillet. Repeat with remaining oil and polenta slices.

3. Arrange polenta on serving platter. Top with tomato-bean salsa. Sprinkle with cheese; garnish with basil.   *Makes 4 servings*

*Tip

To make your own polenta, bring 4 cups of vegetable broth to a boil in a large saucepan over high heat. Slowly stir in 1 cup uncooked polenta or yellow cornmeal. Reduce heat to low; cook 15 to 20 minutes, stirring frequently, or until mixture is very thick and pulls away from side of pan. (Mixture may be lumpy.) Pour polenta into greased 9×5-inch loaf pan. Cool; cover and refrigerate 2 to 3 hours or until firm. Remove the polenta from the pan and cut it crosswise into 16 slices. Cut slices into triangles, if desired. Proceed as directed in step 2.

Sesame Ginger-Glazed Tofu with Rice

1 package (14 ounces) extra firm tofu
1 cup sesame ginger stir-fry sauce, divided
1 cup uncooked long grain rice
4 medium carrots, chopped (about 1 cup)
4 ounces snow peas, halved (about 1 cup)

1. Slice tofu in half crosswise. Cut each half into 2 triangles. Place tofu triangles in single layer on cutting board between layers of paper towels. Place another cutting board on top to press moisture out of tofu. Let stand about 15 minutes.

2. Pour ½ cup stir-fry sauce into baking dish, spreading to coat bottom. Place tofu over sauce; marinate at room temperature 30 minutes, turning after 15 minutes.

3. Meanwhile, cook rice according to package directions. Keep warm.

4. Spray indoor grill pan with nonstick cooking spray; heat over medium-high heat. Place tofu in pan; grill 6 to 8 minutes or until lightly browned, turning after 4 minutes.

5. Meanwhile, pour remaining ½ cup stir-fry sauce into large nonstick skillet; heat over medium-high heat. Add carrots and snow peas; cook and stir 4 to 6 minutes or until crisp-tender. Add rice; stir to combine.

6. Divide rice mixture between 4 plates; top each with tofu triangle.

Makes 4 servings

Baked Risotto with Asparagus, Spinach & Parmesan

1 tablespoon olive oil
1 cup finely chopped onion
1 cup arborio rice
8 cups (8 to 10 ounces) packed torn stemmed spinach
2 cups vegetable broth
¼ teaspoon salt
¼ teaspoon ground nutmeg
½ cup grated Parmesan cheese, divided
1½ cups diagonally sliced asparagus

1. Preheat oven to 400°F. Spray 13×9-inch baking dish with nonstick cooking spray.

2. Heat olive oil in large skillet over medium-high heat. Add onion; cook and stir 4 minutes or until tender. Add rice; stir to coat with oil.

3. Stir in spinach, a handful at a time, adding more as it wilts. Add broth, salt and nutmeg. Reduce heat and simmer 7 minutes. Stir in ¼ cup cheese.

4. Transfer to prepared baking dish. Cover tightly; bake 15 minutes.

5. Remove from oven; stir in asparagus. Sprinkle with remaining ¼ cup cheese. Cover; bake 15 minutes or until liquid is absorbed.

Makes 6 servings

Rice, Cheese & Bean Enchiladas

1 (2-cup) bag UNCLE BEN'S® Boil-in-Bag Rice
4 cups shredded zucchini, drained (2 medium)
1 tablespoon reduced-sodium taco sauce mix
1 can (15 ounces) pinto beans, rinsed and drained
1 can (10 ounces) reduced-fat, reduced-sodium cream of mushroom soup
1 can (8 ounces) diced green chilies
12 (8-inch) flour tortillas
2 cups (8 ounces) reduced-fat Mexican cheese blend, divided

1. Prepare rice following package directions.

2. Combine zucchini and taco sauce mix in large nonstick skillet. Cook and stir zucchini 5 minutes. Add beans, soup, chilies and rice. Bring to a boil.

3. Spray 13×9-inch microwavable baking dish with nonstick cooking spray. Spoon about ½ cup of rice mixture onto center of each tortilla. Top with 2 tablespoons cheese. Roll up to enclose filling; place in baking dish. Sprinkle remaining cheese over enchiladas. Microwave at HIGH 4 minutes or until cheese is melted.   *Makes 6 servings*

Serving Suggestion: Serve with sliced mango or orange sections.

Buckwheat with Zucchini and Mushrooms

1½ to 2 tablespoons olive oil
1 cup sliced mushrooms
1 medium zucchini, cut into ½-inch dice
1 medium onion, chopped
1 clove garlic, minced
¾ cup buckwheat
¼ teaspoon dried thyme
¼ teaspoon salt
⅛ teaspoon black pepper
1¼ cups vegetable broth
Lemon wedges (optional)

1. Heat oil in large nonstick skillet over medium heat. Add mushrooms, zucchini, onion and garlic. Cook and stir 7 to 10 minutes or until vegetables are tender. Stir in buckwheat, thyme, salt and pepper. Cook and stir 2 minutes.

2. Add broth; bring to a boil. Cover; reduce heat to low. Cook 10 to 13 minutes or until liquid is absorbed and buckwheat is tender. Remove from heat; let stand, covered, 5 minutes. Serve with lemon wedges.

Makes 4 to 6 servings

*Tip

Although buckwheat is technically not a grain (it's the fruit of a leafy plant), it is used like other grains in cooking. Unpolished buckwheat kernels, called groats, and ground kernels, called buckwheat grits, are available in health food stores. Toasted groats, known as kasha, are also available. Buckwheat has a strong, nutty flavor that is more pronounced when toasted.

Black Bean Vegetarian Chili
(p. 134)

Lentil Stew over Couscous
(p. 128)

Edamame Frittata
(p. 124)

Chickpea Vegetable Curry
(p. 138)

Luscious Legumes

Edamame Frittata

2 tablespoons olive oil
½ cup frozen shelled edamame
⅓ cup frozen corn
¼ cup chopped shallot (1 shallot)
5 eggs
¾ teaspoon freshly ground Italian herb mix or Italian seasoning
½ teaspoon salt
½ teaspoon black pepper
¼ cup chopped green onions (about 4)
½ cup crumbled goat cheese

1. Preheat broiler. Heat olive oil in large broilerproof skillet over medium-high heat. Add edamame, corn and shallots. Cook and stir 6 to 8 minutes or until shallots are brown and edamame is hot.

2. Meanwhile, beat eggs, seasoning, salt and pepper in medium bowl. Stir in green onions. Pour egg mixture over vegetables in skillet. Sprinkle with cheese. Cook over medium heat 5 to 7 minutes or until eggs are set on bottom, lifting up mixture to allow uncooked portion to flow underneath.

3. Broil 6 inches from heat about 1 minute or until top is puffy and golden. Loosen frittata from skillet with spatula; slide onto small platter. Cut into wedges to serve. *Makes 4 servings*

Black Bean
Cakes

1 can (about 15 ounces) black beans, rinsed and drained
¼ cup all-purpose flour
¼ cup chopped fresh cilantro
2 tablespoons plain yogurt or sour cream
1 tablespoon chili powder
2 cloves garlic, minced
1 tablespoon vegetable oil
Salsa

1. Place beans in medium bowl; mash with fork or potato masher until almost smooth, leaving some beans in larger pieces. Stir in flour, cilantro, yogurt, chili powder and garlic. Shape bean mixture into 8 patties.

2. Heat oil in large nonstick skillet over medium-high heat. Cook patties 6 to 8 minutes or until hot and lightly browned, turning once. Serve with salsa.   *Makes 4 servings*

*Tip

Mexican-inspired food offers vegetarians many tasty choices for snacks and entrées. For a great snack or appetizer, serve theses cakes with salsa, sour cream and guacamole. Or, serve them for dinner with a prepared Spanish rice pilaf mix and a salad of chopped fresh tomatoes, onions and shredded lettuce.

Lentil Stew over Couscous

Prep Time: 10 minutes • **Cook Time:** 8 to 9 hours (LOW)

3 cups dried lentils (1 pound), sorted and rinsed
3 cups water
1 can (about 14 ounces) diced tomatoes
1 can (about 14 ounces) vegetable broth
1 large onion, chopped
1 green bell pepper, chopped
4 stalks celery, chopped
1 medium carrot, halved lengthwise and sliced
2 cloves garlic, chopped
1 teaspoon dried marjoram
¼ teaspoon black pepper
1 tablespoon olive oil
1 tablespoon cider vinegar
4½ to 5 cups hot cooked couscous
    Carrot curls (optional)
    Celery leaves (optional)

Slow Cooker Directions

1. Combine lentils, water, tomatoes, broth, onion, bell pepper, celery, carrot, garlic, marjoram and black pepper in slow cooker; stir. Cover; cook on LOW 8 to 9 hours or until vegetables are tender.

2. Stir in olive oil and vinegar. Serve over couscous. Garnish with carrot curls and celery leaves. *Makes 12 servings*

Tip: Lentil stew keeps well in the refrigerator for up to 1 week. Stew can also be frozen in an airtight container up to three months.

Vegetarian Split Pea Soup

2 cups USA split peas, rinsed
2 quarts water
1 cup sliced celery
½ cup diced onion
1 cup chopped carrots
1 cup diced potato
1 clove garlic, minced
1 bay leaf
¼ cup fresh parsley, snipped
½ teaspoon oregano, crushed
½ teaspoon basil, crushed
1 teaspoon dried Italian seasoning
½ teaspoon salt
Pinch cayenne

Combine all ingredients in a Dutch oven. Bring to a boil.

Reduce heat, cover and simmer 1 hour or until split peas are cooked through. Remove bay leaf before serving. *Makes 10 servings*

Favorite recipe from **USA Dry Pea & Lentil Council**

Falafel Patties with Cucumber Relish

2 boxes (6 ounces each) dry vegetarian falafel mix (2½ cups)
½ cup millet
2⅔ cups cold water
2 teaspoons olive oil
1 cup chopped seeded cucumber
1 cup chopped fresh tomato
1 cup plain yogurt
3 tablespoons chopped fresh mint

1. For falafel patties, combine falafel mix and millet in large bowl. Stir in water. Let stand 10 minutes. Shape mixture into 12 (½-inch-thick) patties.

2. Heat 1 teaspoon oil in large nonstick skillet over medium-high heat until hot. Add 6 patties; cook over medium heat 5 to 6 minutes or until light brown, turning once. Remove from skillet and keep warm. Repeat with remaining oil and patties.

3. For relish, combine cucumber, tomato, yogurt and mint in small bowl. Serve falafel patties with relish.   *Makes 6 servings*

*Tip

These versatile vegetarian patties can be served as an appetizer, sandwich or entrée. To make sandwiches, stuff pita bread with 2 or 3 patties, cucumber relish, lettuce, chopped red onion and feta cheese. For an entrée, serve 3 or 4 patties with rice pilaf, hummus and a salad of greens, olives, feta and balsamic vinaigrette.

Lentil Rice Curry

2 tablespoons olive oil
1 cup sliced green onions
3 cloves garlic, minced
2 tablespoons minced fresh ginger
2 teaspoons curry powder
½ teaspoon ground cumin
½ teaspoon ground turmeric
3 cups water
1 can (about 14 ounces) stewed tomatoes, undrained
½ teaspoon salt
1 cup uncooked red lentils, sorted and rinsed
1 large head cauliflower (about 1¼ pounds), broken into florets
1 tablespoon lemon juice
Hot cooked rice

1. Heat oil in large saucepan over medium heat until hot. Add onions, garlic, ginger, curry, cumin and turmeric; cook and stir 5 minutes. Add water, tomatoes and salt; bring to a boil over high heat.

2. Add lentils to saucepan. Reduce heat to low. Cover and simmer 35 to 40 minutes or until lentils are tender.

3. Add cauliflower and lemon juice. Cover and simmer 8 to 10 minutes or until cauliflower is tender.

4. Serve with rice. *Makes 6 servings*

Black Bean Vegetarian Chili

1 tablespoon olive oil
2 onions, finely chopped, divided
1 green bell pepper, diced
1 teaspoon ground cumin
1 teaspoon minced garlic
4 cans (about 15 ounces each) black beans, rinsed and drained
1 can (15 ounces) corn, drained
1 can (about 14 ounces) diced tomatoes
1 can (6 ounces) tomato paste plus 3 cans water
1 to 2 canned chipotle peppers,* stemmed and diced
½ teaspoon salt
½ teaspoon black pepper
Sour cream
Shredded cheese

Chipotle peppers come in 7-ounce cans packed in adobo sauce. Use 1 pepper for mildly spicy chili, 2 for very spicy. Freeze unused peppers and sauce in small freezer food storage bags for later use.

1. Heat olive oil in Dutch oven until hot. Reserve ½ cup chopped onions. Add remaining onions and bell pepper to Dutch oven; cook and stir 5 minutes or until soft. Add cumin; cook and stir about 10 seconds. Add garlic; cook and stir 1 minute.

2. Stir in black beans, corn, tomatoes, tomato paste, water, chipotle peppers, salt and black pepper. Bring to a boil. Reduce heat; simmer 30 minutes.

3. Serve with reserved onions, sour cream and shredded cheese.

Makes 8 servings

Indian-Style
Red Lentils & Chickpeas

2 teaspoons olive oil
1 small onion *or* 2 large shallots, chopped
½ cup thinly sliced carrots
1 can (about 14 ounces) vegetable broth
1 cup uncooked red or brown lentils, sorted and rinsed
¾ cup water
1 teaspoon garam masala or curry powder
¼ teaspoon red pepper flakes (optional)
1 can (15 ounces) chickpeas, rinsed and drained
½ cup crumbled feta cheese
2 tablespoons chopped fresh cilantro

1. Heat oil in large saucepan over medium heat. Add onion and carrots; cook 5 minutes, stirring occasionally. Add broth, lentils, water, garam masala and pepper flakes, if desired; bring to a boil. Reduce heat; cover and simmer 15 minutes (20 minutes for brown lentils) or until lentils are just tender.

2. Stir in chickpeas; cook until heated through. Ladle into bowls; top with cheese and cilantro. *Makes 4 servings*

Note: Garam masala is a blend of spices often used in Indian cooking. It usually includes black pepper, dried chili peppers, cardamom, coriander, cumin and cinnamon.

Stuffed Squash with Black Beans

1 acorn squash (2 pounds), quartered and seeded
1½ ounces pine nuts
1 tablespoon olive oil
1 cup chopped onion
1 medium red bell pepper, chopped
1 teaspoon ground cinnamon
¼ teaspoon ground allspice (optional)
1 cup canned black beans, rinsed and drained
¼ cup raisins
1 teaspoon sugar (optional)
¼ teaspoon salt
2 ounces crumbled goat cheese or feta cheese

1. Place ½ cup water in 8-inch square microwavable baking dish. Place squash skin side up in dish. Cover with plastic wrap. Microwave on HIGH 12 minutes or until tender.

2. Meanwhile, heat medium nonstick skillet over medium-high heat. Add pine nuts. Cook and stir 1 minute or until lightly browned. Remove to plate.

3. Heat oil in large skillet over medium heat. Add onion and bell pepper. Cook and stir 5 minutes or until beginning to brown. Add cinnamon and allspice, if desired; cook and stir 30 seconds. Add beans, raisins, sugar, if desired, and salt. Gradually stir in ½ cup water. Remove from heat. Cover; let stand 2 minutes.

4. Remove squash to serving platter. Spoon bean mixture over each quarter. Sprinkle with pine nuts and cheese.   *Makes 4 servings*

Chickpea Vegetable Curry

1 tablespoon olive or canola oil
1 large onion, chopped
1 teaspoon minced garlic
1 tablespoon curry powder
1 can (12 ounces) evaporated skimmed milk plus 1 can water
½ teaspoon salt
¼ teaspoon coconut extract
1½ cups sliced carrots
2 cups cubed peeled potatoes
1 can (15 ounces) chickpeas, rinsed and drained
1 cup frozen cut green beans
6 cups cooked rice
Toppings: prepared chutney, chopped peanuts, golden raisins and chopped green onions

1. Heat oil in large saucepan over medium-high heat. Add onion; cook and stir 5 minutes or until soft. Add garlic; cook and stir 1 minute. Stir in curry powder.

2. Add milk, water, salt and coconut extract. Bring to a boil. Add carrots; cook 10 minutes, stirring occasionally.

3. Add potatoes; cook 10 minutes, stirring occasionally. Add chickpeas; cook 10 minutes.

4. Stir in beans; cook 5 minutes or until vegetables are tender. Serve over rice with desired toppings.   *Makes 6 servings*

The publisher would like to thank the companies and organizations listed below for the use of their recipes in this publication.

Cream of Wheat® Cereal

MASTERFOODS USA

Ortega®, A Division of B&G Foods, Inc.

Reckitt Benckiser Inc.

Riviana Foods Inc.

Unilever

USA Dry Pea & Lentil Council

VOLUME MEASUREMENTS (dry)

$1/8$ teaspoon = 0.5 mL
$1/4$ teaspoon = 1 mL
$1/2$ teaspoon = 2 mL
$3/4$ teaspoon = 4 mL
1 teaspoon = 5 mL
1 tablespoon = 15 mL
2 tablespoons = 30 mL
$1/4$ cup = 60 mL
$1/3$ cup = 75 mL
$1/2$ cup = 125 mL
$2/3$ cup = 150 mL
$3/4$ cup = 175 mL
1 cup = 250 mL
2 cups = 1 pint = 500 mL
3 cups = 750 mL
4 cups = 1 quart = 1 L

VOLUME MEASUREMENTS (fluid)

1 fluid ounce (2 tablespoons) = 30 mL
4 fluid ounces ($1/2$ cup) = 125 mL
8 fluid ounces (1 cup) = 250 mL
12 fluid ounces ($1 1/2$ cups) = 375 mL
16 fluid ounces (2 cups) = 500 mL

WEIGHTS (mass)

$1/2$ ounce = 15 g
1 ounce = 30 g
3 ounces = 90 g
4 ounces = 120 g
8 ounces = 225 g
10 ounces = 285 g
12 ounces = 360 g
16 ounces = 1 pound = 450 g

DIMENSIONS

$1/16$ inch = 2 mm
$1/8$ inch = 3 mm
$1/4$ inch = 6 mm
$1/2$ inch = 1.5 cm
$3/4$ inch = 2 cm
1 inch = 2.5 cm

OVEN TEMPERATURES

250°F = 120°C
275°F = 140°C
300°F = 150°C
325°F = 160°C
350°F = 180°C
375°F = 190°C
400°F = 200°C
425°F = 220°C
450°F = 230°C

BAKING PAN SIZES

Utensil	Size in Inches/Quarts	Metric Volume	Size in Centimeters
Baking or Cake Pan (square or rectangular)	$8 \times 8 \times 2$	2 L	$20 \times 20 \times 5$
	$9 \times 9 \times 2$	2.5 L	$23 \times 23 \times 5$
	$12 \times 8 \times 2$	3 L	$30 \times 20 \times 5$
	$13 \times 9 \times 2$	3.5 L	$33 \times 23 \times 5$
Loaf Pan	$8 \times 4 \times 3$	1.5 L	$20 \times 10 \times 7$
	$9 \times 5 \times 3$	2 L	$23 \times 13 \times 7$
Round Layer Cake Pan	$8 \times 1 1/2$	1.2 L	20×4
	$9 \times 1 1/2$	1.5 L	23×4
Pie Plate	$8 \times 1 1/4$	750 mL	20×3
	$9 \times 1 1/4$	1 L	23×3
Baking Dish or Casserole	1 quart	1 L	—
	$1 1/2$ quart	1.5 L	—
	2 quart	2 L	—